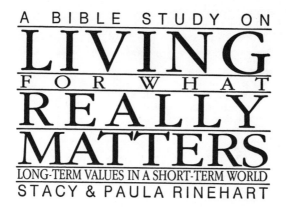

A BIBLE STUDY ON

LIVING

FOR WHAT

REALLY

MATTERS

LONG-TERM VALUES IN A SHORT-TERM WORLD

STACY & PAULA RINEHART

NAVPRESS ●

A MINISTRY OF THE NAVIGATORS

P.O. Box 6000, Colorado Springs, Colorado 80934

The Navigators is an international Christian organization. Jesus Christ gave His followers the Great Commission to go and make disciples (Matthew 28:19). The aim of The Navigators is to help fulfill that commission by multiplying laborers for Christ in every nation.

NavPress is the publishing ministry of The Navigators. NavPress publications are tools to help Christians grow. Although publications alone cannot make disciples or change lives, they can help believers learn biblical discipleship, and apply what they learn to their lives and ministries.

Cover illustration: Mark Chickinelli

Unless otherwise identified, Scripture quotations are from the *New American Standard Bible* (NASB), © The Lockman Foundation 1960, 1962, 1963, 1968, 1971, 1972, 1973, 1975, 1977.

Printed in the United States of America

Contents

Authors

Stacy Rinehart holds a Doctor of Ministry degree from Trinity Evangelical Divinity School and a Master of Theology degree from Dallas Theological Seminary. He is the director of the Leadership Development Institute at Glen Eyrie in Colorado Springs, Colorado. Previously he served as the Navigator representative in Tulsa, Oklahoma. He also directed the Navigator student ministry at Oklahoma State University. Stacy came into contact with The Navigators at Fort Benning, Georgia, while serving as an officer in the U.S. Army.

Paula Rinehart is a graduate of the University of Tennessee, where she was involved with The Navigators.

Stacy and Paula are the authors of the award-winning NavPress book *Choices.* They live in Colorado Springs with their two children, Allison and Brady.

How to Use
This Bible Study

A Bible Study on Living for What Really Matters is for use either alone or with the book *Living for What Really Matters*, also written by Stacy and Paula Rinehart. The study is suitable for personal use, for Sunday school classes, or for home Bible study groups. The twelve chapters in the study correspond with chapters 1 through 12 in the book. You may want to read each chapter in the book as part of your completion of each chapter in the study.

Introduction

One of the greatest contrasts in Scripture consists of man's transient nature, which is no more lasting than today's table flower, and the living, eternal God. The Bible is the window in this ramshackle structure of time through which we can glimpse eternity.

In those glimpses, of which this Bible study consists, the means for discerning the crucial from the inconsequential becomes clear. God's Word is the only reliable aid for determining what is truly significant in life.

In the Bible's pages are recognizable men and women who have grappled with the visceral tugs of this world's allures. The basic issues of life remain the same in every age. For this reason, we encourage you to give yourself wholeheartedly to the study of the Book, the eternal Word, which along with the Holy Spirit, is your surest guide as you move through the crumbling city of man to the everlasting city of God.

1
Heaven Can't Wait

John Wesley, a great English preacher (1703-1791), said that we stand on an "isthmus of life" between the two boundless oceans of eternity. To see this life within the larger, dominant realm of eternity; to willingly choose the eternal over the temporal and the immediate; this is what it means to have an eternal perspective.

1. a. Read 1 Peter 1:3-9 and consider how Peter relates the hope of eternity to the present.

_____

_____

_____

_____

b. How does he describe this "living hope" we have been born again to?

_____

_____

_____

_____

_____

c. What effect could this have on our walk with God?

_____

_____

_____

_____

_____

_____

_____

_____

2. a. How would you describe your thoughts about eternity before you became a Christian? Did you, for example, think the hope of Heaven was necessary only for weak people who couldn't face the harsh realities of the present?

_____

_____

_____

_____

_____

_____

_____

_____

b. How has your thinking changed? What bearing do you feel
   eternity and Heaven should have on a Christian's life?

_____

_____

_____

_____

_____

_____

_____

_____

3. It is to our benefit to recapture a sense of the eternal glory
   God has called us to. In Romans 8:18-25, Paul records a
   number of things we can look forward to.

   a. What are those?

_____

_____

_____

_____

_____

_____

_____

b. How does the present compare with the future?

_____

_____

_____

_____

_____

_____

_____

_____

c. Look at verses 24 and 25 of Romans 8. Here Paul speaks of hope as a confident expectation of the glorious future he described in previous verses. Why do you think he speaks of waiting with *perseverance* for what we do not yet see?

_____

_____

_____

_____

_____

_____

_____

d. What enables a Christian to persevere with his eyes fixed firmly on the hope of eternal glory? Consider these verses as you answer this question:

Romans 15:4 _____

_____

_____

Hebrews 6:11-12 _____

_____

_____

Hebrews 10:23-24 _____

_____

_____

4. Great men of the faith have always lived with eternity in mind.

a. According to the passages that follow, how did Abraham and Moses exemplify their faith? What were they willing to do in the present?

Abraham—Hebrews 11:8-10 _____

_____

_____

_____

_____

_____

13

_____

_____

_____

_____

_____

_____

_____

b. In what ways does your life demonstrate a willingness to
   sacrifice, or forgo, the temporal for the eternal, for God's
   Kingdom?

_____

_____

_____

_____

_____

_____

_____

5. There is no neutral ground in eternity. C.S. Lewis, an English writer (1898-1963), said that each of us is on our way to
   becoming either an everlasting splendor or an immortal
   horror.

a. Paraphrase the following verses to contrast the future of the unregenerate (godless) person and the future of the person who knows Christ.

The unregenerate person

Isaiah 2:19 _____

_____

_____

_____

2 Thessalonians 1:8-9 _____

_____

_____

_____

The person who knows Christ

Isaiah 25:8-9 _____

_____

_____

_____

Revelation 21:3-4 _____

_____

_____

_____

b. How does the contemplation of such a future affect your present motivations?

_____

_____

_____

_____

_____

_____

c. Even as we anticipate our joy in being with Christ, what should be our attitude toward those around us who don't know Him?

_____

_____

_____

_____

6. Union with Christ in Heaven will fulfill our innermost longings for security, intimacy, significance, and wholeness.

a. Complete this sentence: At this point in life, my greatest unmet need—my deepest sense of longing—is

_____

_____

_____

_____

b. Now consider and paraphrase Psalm 73:25.

_____

_____

_____

_____

_____

_____

_____

c. Was the psalmist carelessly glossing over the needs and desires in his life? What do you think he meant when he said he desired nothing on earth besides the Lord?

_____

_____

_____

_____

_____

_____

_____

7. Christ exemplified an eternal perspective, which is revealed in John 13:1-5.

a. In what way does His grasp of eternal realities affect His behavior in this instance? What does His understanding enable Him to do?

_____

_____

_____

_____

_____

_____

b. What principle does this passage teach about the relationship between an eternal perspective and your self-image?

_____

_____

_____

_____

_____

_____

_____

8. The New Testament writers consistently point to the return of Christ and the joys of Heaven as our motivation to obey God and follow Him wholeheartedly in the present. Knowing that Christ's atoning work makes Heaven's joys possible is never an opportunity for license and halfheartedness.

Look closely at these verses. What response does each one encourage, and what motivation is given for that response?

Colossians 3:4-5 _____

_____

_____

_____

_____

2 Peter 3:10-11,14 _____

_____

_____

_____

_____

1 John 3:2-3 _____

_____

_____

_____

_____

9. a. As you worked on this chapter, did a particular hindrance come to mind that keeps you from living now in the light of eternity?

_____

_____

_____

_____

_____

b. What steps can you take to remove that hindrance?

_____

_____

_____

_____

_____

_____

_____

_____

_____

2
Competing Allegiances

Throughout the ages, Christians have struggled to live distinctively for Christ in the midst of the world's influence. The question of our loyalty is at stake. Will we allow our lives, in the deep areas of motives, attitudes, and values, to reflect the image of the One whose love redeemed us? Or will we be content to give Him lip service while we let the world mold our thinking and behavior?

1. History, as Tolstoy said, is shaped by the passions and dreams of the masses, by what seizes the mind and heart of the average person. Looking as objectively as possible at your culture, what would you say are the aspirations and goals of the average person?

_____

_____

_____

_____

_____

_____

_____

_____

2. Christians in every generation are beset by the temptation to define true spirituality in terms of adherence to an external code of legalistic behavior. Christian schools of the second century encouraged those who were serious about following Christ to forsake wearing colored clothes, sleeping on a soft pillow, playing musical instruments, eating white bread, shaving, or indulging in a warm bath!

a. What might be included in a list of legalistic taboos today?

_____

_____

_____

_____

_____

_____

b. Why do you think we are so greatly tempted to define spirituality using a specific, superficial list of do's and dont's?

_____

_____

_____

_____

_____

_____

_____

3. In Colossians 2, Paul deals with three common substitutions for true spirituality:

Legalism (verses 16-17)—establishing manmade rules in matters that should be left to the discretion of the individual before God.

Mysticism (verses 18-19)—in this sense, taking inordinate pride in private knowledge of God and a subjective experience of Him.

Asceticism (verses 20-23)—basing spirituality on the denial of the flesh and gratification of the physical senses.

Read the verses given above to complete the chart.

	Paraphrase the thought.	How is this insufficient?	What is a similar substitution today?
Legalism			
Mysticism			
Asceticism			

4. In our efforts to live distinctively Christian lives, Christ must always be central. Read Colossians 3:1-4, keeping in mind that Paul has just explained in chapter 2 the insufficiencies of legalism, mysticism, and asceticism.

   a. What does Paul suggest in chapter 3 as the path toward genuine spirituality?

   _____

   _____

   _____

   _____

   b. Why could verse 4 be a particular encouragement?

   _____

   _____

   _____

   c. In addressing the question of true spirituality, Paul describes characteristics that should decrease as we continually seek God. What are they? Colossians 3:5,8-10

   _____

   _____

   _____

   _____

   _____

d. A changed life is manifested primarily in *relationships* with people. It can't be confined to the purely private arena of life. How does Paul describe this renewal in verses 12-17?

_____

_____

_____

_____

5. The world is characterized in biblical terms as fleeting, temporal, and passing away.

a. Read 1 Peter 1:18-19 and 23. How does our redemption contrast with the world as the Bible describes it?

_____

_____

_____

_____

_____

_____

b. How should this affect the way we live for God?

_____

_____

_____

_____

_____

c. Peter says in verse 18 that we were redeemed from our futile way of life that we inherited from our forefathers. In terms of attitudes, values, and behavior, how would you describe your futile way of life?

_____

_____

_____

_____

_____

6. Worldliness is first of all a matter of adopting a mind-set, which then influences a person's behavior. Listed below are some common "worldly" attitudes and corresponding biblical responses. Consider the passage listed for each attitude and then write a biblical response to that attitude. (You might also think of other attitudes and verses.)

a. Keep all your options open so you will be free to change your mind whenever you want to. Matthew 7:13-14

_____

_____

_____

_____

b. You shouldn't have to struggle; in fact, avoid pain at all costs. 1 Peter 4:12-13

_____

_____

_____

c. Your lifestyle should be upwardly mobile, becoming more comfortable and affluent with each passing year. Philippians 4:11-13

_____

_____

_____

d. Above all, look out for yourself—no one else will. John 13:3-5

_____

_____

_____

7. a. Read John 12:42-43. How does an inordinate desire for men's approval foster compromise with the world?

_____

_____

_____

b. Read the contrasting description of Peter and the disciples after Christ arose, recorded in Acts 5:27-29 and 41-42. What attitudes caused these men to be willing to risk condemnation and reproach?

_____

_____

_____

_____

8. Read James 4:1-6, in which the writer deals with spirituality in terms of deep issues of the heart like envy and lust.

    a. How do envy and lust produce quarrels and breed friendship with the world?

_____

_____

_____

_____

_____

    b. Why does God consider friendship with the world to be hostility toward Him?

_____

_____

_____

_____

9. Sometimes our lives are characterized more by *godlessness* (leaving God out of the picture) than by the sheer ungodliness of a pagan lifestyle. Read James 4:13-15. How is it "worldly" to make decisions without praying in openness and dependence upon the Lord?

_____

_____

_____

_____

10. a. Abraham's nephew, Lot, lived in the midst of the corruption of Sodom and Gomorrah. Read Genesis 13:8-13, which describes the manner in which Lot made his decision to settle in Sodom. What were the deciding factors for Lot?

_____

_____

_____

_____

What did he neglect to consider or do in the process of making his choice?

_____

_____

_____

_____

b. When God's messengers came to warn Lot to take his family and flee Sodom before destruction came, he hesitated. Read Genesis 19:16. How did God demonstrate long-suffering compassion toward Lot?

_____

_____

_____

_____

_____

c. Have you ever been like Lot, so that God in His compassion had to take you by the hand and pull you out? How has that experience affected your obedience?

_____

_____

_____

_____

11. The potential for "turning aside" exists for every Christian at any point in his life. Read 1 Samuel 12:21-22 and 24.

a. What constitutes turning aside for you?

_____

_____

_____

b. How does Samuel describe the things we turn aside to?

_____

_____

_____

c. What are some "great things" God has done for you?

_____

_____

_____

_____

12. Sometimes we succumb to the illusion that the world can meet our needs; that more money or job advancement or sharper clothes can bring us what we long for.

a. What situations or memories or thought patterns increase your interest in the world?

_____

_____

_____

_____

b. Considering the verses you have studied so far, what is the way out? (Notice the active verbs in some of the verses: *flee, seek, grow, turn aside.*)

_____

_____

_____

_____

c. As you consider the implications of your study, how would you define worldliness? Conversely, what constitutes true spirituality?

_____

_____

_____

_____

_____

13. As you reflect on your thoughts and answers in this study, is God leading you to a particular course of action? If so, what?

_____

_____

_____

_____

_____

_____

_____

_____

3
A Heart for People

This world is teeming with a wide assortment of people—among them, blond Scandinavians, Pygmies, swarthy Italians, big-boned Russians, and petite Japanese—people for whom Christ died, of whom some from every tribe and tongue and people and nation will be represented in Heaven. We cannot open the Scriptures without catching a glimpse of God's heart for people.

1. God made us in His image and bestowed on us a measure of His glory. The Hebrew word for *glory* means "weightiness"; it denotes God as having a substantial, or "solid," existence.

   a. Read Romans 1:23. What happens to that glory when a person turns away from God?

   _____

   _____

   _____

   _____

   b. Now look at 2 Corinthians 3:18. For what does this verse give you hope?

   _____

   _____

   _____

What is the means of accomplishing that?

_____

_____

_____

_____

2. To believe that God can change a person's natural tendencies is fundamentally necessary in order to see spiritual progress and growth.

   a. What happens if you consciously or unconsciously accept the idea that your personality is determined by hereditary and environmental forces totally beyond your control?

   _____

   _____

   _____

   _____

   _____

   _____

   b. How, in practical ways, can this attitude affect your response toward other people?

   _____

   _____

   _____

   _____

3. The Bible is full of the imagery of change and transformation, giving repeated evidence that God is at work in our lives. What truths do the following images teach? What implications do you see for your life?

   a. A field (Isaiah 61:3, 1 Corinthians 3:9)

   The truth _____

   _____

   _____

   _____

   The implication _____

   _____

   _____

   _____

   b. A spiritual house (1 Peter 2:5)

   The truth _____

   _____

   _____

   _____

   The implication _____

   _____

   _____

   _____

c. A tree (Jeremiah 17:7-8)

The truth _____

_____

_____

_____

The implication _____

_____

_____

_____

d. A bride (Ephesians 5:25-27, Revelation 19:6-8)

The truth _____

_____

_____

_____

_____

The implication _____

_____

_____

_____

4. Read and consider Isaiah 61:1-3.

    a. How would you record what God desires to do in a person's life?

_____

_____

_____

_____

_____

    b. Look especially at the last image in verse 3, "oaks of righteousness." How would you explain that scriptural image of spiritual maturity?

_____

_____

_____

_____

5. In 2 Corinthians 5, the Apostle Paul writes about reconciliation. We have been reconciled to God *and* given the ministry of reconciling others to Him.

    a. Look at verses 14-16. What does it mean to regard someone from a worldly point of view?

_____

_____

_____

_____

b. How does that affect our ability to effectively take part in a ministry of reconciliation?

_____

_____

_____

_____

_____

_____

_____

6. In his epistles, Paul repeatedly revealed his concern and care about those he shepherded spiritually. He spoke of being "in labor" until Christ was formed in them (Galatians 4:19).

a. Read 1 Corinthians 4:10-13 and 2 Corinthians 11:23-30. What do you discover Paul was willing to do in order to help people spiritually?

_____

_____

_____

_____

_____

_____

_____

b. In 1 Thessalonians 2:1-12, how does Paul describe his motivations and his approach to the people he dealt with?

_____

_____

_____

_____

_____

_____

c. This same man had passively watched those who stoned Stephen to death (Acts 7:54-60). How does this affect your thoughts concerning changed lives?

_____

_____

_____

_____

_____

7. a. Read Exodus 3:7 and Matthew 9:36. What principle of developing a heart for people can you find in God's example?

_____

_____

_____

_____

b. Look at 1 Kings 3:9, where Solomon perceived his need for an understanding heart. What can you learn from him?

_____

_____

_____

_____

c. How would you apply the implications of the verses in questions a and b?

_____

_____

_____

_____

_____

_____

_____

8. God uses the trials and difficulties of life to conform us to the image of Christ.

a. Read Romans 5:3-5. Why does Paul exult in tribulations?

_____

_____

_____

_____

b. How does one quality bring about another quality?

_____

_____

_____

_____

c. Which of the qualities listed by Paul are most appealing to you, and why?

_____

_____

_____

_____

9. a. How did Paul view his trials and difficulties?

2 Corinthians 1:4 _____

_____

_____

_____

2 Corinthians 4:10-12 _____

_____

_____

_____

2 Timothy 2:10 _____

_____

_____

_____

_____

b. What trials and difficulties in your life has God used in
recent years to help others?

_____

_____

_____

_____

_____

_____

10. a. As described in Isaiah 58:1-12, what does it mean to invest
your life in other people?

_____

_____

_____

_____

_____

_____

b. What benefits does Isaiah mention that result from your willingness to invest your life in people?

_____

_____

_____

_____

_____

_____

_____

c. Each of us has benefited from the faithfulness and concern of other people who have been willing to pray for us, teach us, model Christianity before us, and then nurture us in the faith. Who are those people in your life, and what contributions did they make? Have you ever thanked them?

_____

_____

_____

_____

_____

_____

_____

_____

d. What choices have you made in light of the eternal worth
   of another person?

_____

_____

_____

_____

_____

_____

11. As you worked through this study, did God bring anyone to
    mind? Perhaps you might share your faith with that person
    or invest time in spiritually nurturing him or her. Who is on
    your mind, and what steps could you take?

_____

_____

_____

_____

_____

_____

_____

_____

4
A Sense of Significance

Christians are caught between two unyielding concepts of man. The first, biological determinism, insists that the individual is a machine programmed to act in a prescribed manner. What real good can come of him? The second, humanism, portrays man with infinite potential on his way toward perfection.

In contrast to both, Christianity offers a third, biblical alternative. The individual IS great . . . but he is also lost. The questions we must ask and answer, then, are these: What does God think of me? How should I think of myself?

1. Jacques Monod, a contemporary biologist who wrote the controversial book *Chance and Necessity,* says that it's time to accept the fact that we are alone in a universe of unfeeling immensity, out of which we emerged only by chance. We have no destiny, no purpose, and no significance. There is, therefore, no basis for laws, duty, or morality.

Contrast Monod's assertions with the truth of an ancient, profound book—the Bible. Paraphrase the following verses and explain how they oppose Monod's outlook on life. Also include any other references or illustrations from Scripture that you feel apply.

Job 23:1 _____

_____

_____

_____

_____

Psalm 139:13-16 _____

_____

_____

_____

_____

Isaiah 43:1-2 and 7 _____

_____

_____

_____

_____

2 Timothy 1:9 _____

_____

_____

_____

_____

2. To be forgotten, out of mind, is the lowest point of insignifi-
cance. At one point in his life David lamented, "I am forgotten as a dead man, out of mind" (Psalm 31:12). Conversely,
to be remembered, considered, kept in mind, is an inexpress-
ible honor.

a. What do the following verses teach about your significance to God?

Psalm 139:17-18 _____

_____

_____

_____

Isaiah 44:21 _____

_____

_____

_____

Isaiah 49:15-16 _____

_____

_____

_____

b. What truth about our significance is expressed in Ephesians 1:3-6 and 1 Peter 2:9-10?

_____

_____

_____

_____

_____

_____

c. How does the knowledge that God thinks of you, and thinks well of you in Christ, motivate you in your walk with God?

_____

_____

_____

_____

_____

_____

_____

_____

d. When you struggle with feeling worthless or insignificant, which of these truths have you probably lost sight of?

_____

_____

_____

_____

_____

_____

3. The modern preoccupation with "me" is actually as old as Adam. After he tasted the forbidden fruit, Adam revealed his newly-awakened self-consciousness when he said to God, "*I* heard the sound of Thee in the garden, and *I* was afraid because *I* was naked; so *I* hid myself" (Genesis 3:10).

a. Read Ecclesiastes 11:9 and Isaiah 50:11. What warnings do you find in these verses?

_____

_____

_____

_____

_____

_____

_____

b. Pascal, the seventeenth-century Christian philosopher, said, "It is vain oh men that you seek within yourselves the cure for your miseries. All your insight only leads you to the knowledge that it is not in yourselves that you will discover the true and the good."[1]

He spoke in light of biblical passages such as Jeremiah 17:5-8. Read this passage and record your observations.

	His characteristics	The outcome of his life
The person who trusts in himself or others		
The person who trusts in God		

49

c. How would you complete this thought: I know that I am actively and trusting God, not myself, when I

_____

_____

_____

_____

_____

_____

_____

4. The Scriptures give a seemingly contradictory message about how we are to think of ourselves. On one hand, we are told to affirm our self-worth; on the other, to deny ourselves.

a. What basis for affirmation is seen in these verses?

Romans 8:31-32 _____

_____

_____

_____

_____

1 John 2:1 _____

_____

_____

_____

b. What aspects of myself am I to deny?

Luke 9:23 _____

_____

_____

_____

_____

Galatians 5:24 _____

_____

_____

_____

_____

> The paradox is resolved in the Cross, which is both
> the proof of our value to God and the greatest
> example and picture of self-denial. Thus whatever we
> are by creation and redemption we affirm: our
> rationality, sense of moral obligation, masculinity or
> femininity, our creativity. But whatever we are by the
> Fall, we must deny or turn our backs on: our moral
> perversity, selfishness, malice, our proud autonomy.[2]

5. We follow God more readily when we know of and are
confident in His good purposes for us. In Hebrews 6:13-19,
the writer applys two promises that God gave to Abraham
to his heirs—you and me.

51

a. What are those promises, and what do they mean?

_____

_____

_____

_____

_____

_____

_____

_____

_____

b. What hope do we have as an anchor for our souls?

_____

_____

_____

_____

_____

_____

6. It is easy, in a shortsighted, narcissistic culture, to interpret God's blessings on our lives as meant for us alone. Those blessings have a larger purpose, however.

Look at the lives of three men of the Old Testament—Abraham, Joseph, and David. For what reason does the Bible say God blessed each one? What larger purpose did He have in mind?

	The reason	The larger purpose
Abraham Genesis 12:1-3		
Joseph Genesis 45:5-7		
David 2 Samuel 5:12		

7. God seems to delight in the deliverance of many through the obedience of one.

   a. Read about Moses, Gideon, and David. Then describe what each man felt God had asked him to do, how he responded, and what God brought about as the result.

   Moses

   God's request—Exodus 3:1-10 _____

   _____

   _____

   _____

Moses' response—Exodus 3:11; 4:1,10,13 _____

_____

_____

_____

The result—Exodus 12:31-36_____

_____

_____

_____

Gideon

God's request—Judges 6:11-18_____

_____

_____

_____

Gideon's response—Judges 6:13,15,17 _____

_____

_____

_____

The result—Judges 7:22,24-25 _____

_____

_____

_____

David

God's request—1 Samuel 17:8-11,23 _____

_____

_____

_____

David's response—1 Samuel 17:32-37_____

_____

_____

_____

_____

The result—1 Samuel 17:41-53_____

_____

_____

_____

b. To what would you attribute the difference in David's
confident response?

_____

_____

_____

_____

_____

c. Was God's ability to work in each situation conditional upon the confidence of the person to whom the task was given? Explain your answer.

_____

_____

_____

_____

_____

_____

_____

_____

d. How does this make you feel?

_____

_____

_____

_____

_____

_____

8. God does not value us any more because of our "accomplishments" in serving Him.

a. In 2 Samuel, chapter 9, read the story of Mephibosheth, Jonathan's lame son whom David cared for because of his

friendship with Jonathan. Note all the spiritual parallels
you can find to your relationship with God because of the
work of Christ.

_____

_____

_____

_____

_____

_____

_____

_____

_____

b. If "seeing results" is not proper or sufficient motivation
for serving God, then what is?

Matthew 25:21 _____

_____

_____

_____

Luke 7:7-10 _____

_____

_____

_____

2 Corinthians 5:9 _____

_____

_____

_____

9. In chapter 4 of *Living for What Really Matters*, the authors make this statement: "To find significance, I must lose my life in something greater than myself."

a. What do you think it means to lose your life in "something greater"?

_____

_____

_____

_____

b. How might you apply that truth now or in the future?

_____

_____

_____

_____

_____

_____

NOTES
1. Blaise Pascal, as quoted by Malcolm Muggeridge in *The End of Christendom* (Grand Rapids, Michigan: Eerdmans Publishing Company, 1980), page 12.
2. John Stott, "Am I Supposed to Love Myself or Hate Myself," *Christianity Today*, April 20, 1984, page 26.

5
Taking Aim

We can engage in a host of worthwhile Christian activities and projects, but the real battle for spiritual growth takes place in the hidden arena of ambitions and motives. Fundamentally, the questions we must ask ourselves are, Why do I do what I do? Are the goals that motivate me a reflection of the lordship of Christ over my life?

1. Ambition, that inner reservoir of drive and motivation, can assume many forms. How do the Old Testament people below exemplify unrighteous ambition?

   Eve—Genesis 3:1-6 _____

   _____

   _____

   _____

   _____

   Miriam and Aaron—Numbers 12:1-2,10 _____

   _____

   _____

   _____

   _____

Absalom—2 Samuel 15:1-6 _____

_____

_____

_____

_____

_____

2. The life of Moses is one of contrast. God chose him to stand
   before Pharaohs and to lead His chosen people; yet Moses
   was a truly humble, self-effacing man. What do the two
   scenes in Numbers reveal to you in regard to Moses'
   ambition?

   Numbers 11:27-29 _____

   _____

   _____

   _____

   _____

   _____

   Numbers 12:13 (in light of Miriam's challenge) _____

   _____

   _____

   _____

   _____

   _____

3. The life of Daniel also gives us an example of godly ambition to emulate. The span of his life included falling in and out of favor with three rulers, in the midst of adjusting to the edicts and customs of a foreign land.

Use the verses below to look into Daniel's heart. How would you describe his motives and ambitions?

Daniel 1:8 _____

_____

_____

_____

_____

_____

Daniel 5:17-29 _____

_____

_____

_____

_____

_____

Daniel 6:1-11 _____

_____

_____

_____

_____

4. Contrast selfish ambition and godly wisdom as revealed in James 3:13-18.

	Its characteristics	What it produces
Selfish ambition		
Godly wisdom		

5. What God values is often the opposite of the goals we commonly think are appropriate. According to these verses, what does God consider worthy and valuable?

Jeremiah 9:23-24 _____

_____

_____

_____

Mark 10:35-45 _____

_____

_____

_____

_____

_____

Galatians 1:10 _____

_____

_____

_____

6. Gratitude is fundamental to a righteous desire to please and
serve God alone. David alludes to this as he describes all that
God has done for him in Psalm 40:1-3.

   a. How would you personalize this passage?

_____

_____

_____

_____

_____

_____

_____

   b. What "pit" has God delivered you from or kept you from?

_____

_____

_____

_____

_____

_____

c. What song has He put in your mouth?

_____

_____

_____

_____

_____

_____

_____

d. In Psalm 27:4 David stated his greatest ambition in life. What was it, and what do you think was the basis of his desire?

_____

_____

_____

_____

_____

_____

_____

_____

7. The Apostle Paul recorded the metamorphosis of his goals and ambitions in his letter to the Philippians.

a. Read Philippians 3:1-6. In what areas had Paul achieved a measure of success, giving him cause for pride? (You may want to give these areas more modern labels.)

_____

_____

_____

_____

_____

b. In Philippians 3:8-14, what did Paul reveal to be the goals and desire of his life after he came to Christ?

_____

_____

_____

_____

c. How do you account for such a reversal? Why do you think Paul was able to turn his back on worldly achievements, seeing them in their proper light?

_____

_____

_____

_____

_____

_____

d. Consider your own background and achievements. If you were making a list like Paul, how would yours read?

_____

_____

_____

_____

_____

_____

_____

8. In applying your study of ambition, write a personalized version (as Paul did) of what you would like your ambitions in life to be. (Try to phrase these in specific, rather than general, terms.)

_____

_____

_____

_____

_____

_____

_____

_____

6
*More Than
a Job*

Our work occupies a significantly large percentage of our waking hours. How can we balance that aspect of life, neither relegating it to some spiritual back alley nor allowing ourselves to be consumed by the drive to "get ahead"?

1. a. Contrast the role of work in man's life *before* the Fall and *after* the Fall.

Before—Genesis 1:26,28 and 2:8_____

_____

_____

_____

_____

_____

After—Genesis 3:17-19 _____

_____

_____

_____

_____

_____

b. How do you see the results of the Fall evidenced in the daily world of work?

_____

_____

_____

_____

_____

_____

_____

2. King Solomon struggled in addressing the nature of work.

a. Read Ecclesiastes 2:18-23 and describe his struggle.

_____

_____

_____

_____

b. Now consider Ecclesiastes 2:24-25 and 3:12-13. What point of resolution did Solomon come to?

_____

_____

_____

_____

3. a. According to John 3:6 and Romans 8:5-8, what is the determining factor in making any action—any work—"secular" or "spiritual"?

_____

_____

_____

_____

b. Do you think it is possible to do work that is commonly thought of as "spiritual" in a secular way? Can you give an example?

_____

_____

_____

_____

_____

_____

c. How might you be able to do work commonly thought of as "secular" and consider it spiritual?

_____

_____

_____

_____

_____

4. a. Does God depend on our work in order to keep His universe functioning and His purposes going forward? Consider Isaiah 46:9-10 and Hebrews 4:3-4 as you give your answer.

_____

_____

_____

_____

_____

_____

_____

b. For what reason does man work?

_____

_____

_____

_____

5. What attitudes in work does God encourage and what does He warn against?

2 Chronicles 31:21 _____

_____

_____

_____

Proverbs 18:9 _____

_____

_____

_____

Colossians 3:23 _____

_____

_____

_____

6. a. What reward does God promise for our work, according to 1 Corinthians 15:58 and Ephesians 6:5-8?

_____

_____

_____

_____

_____

b. What would you say constitutes "the work of the Lord"?

_____

_____

_____

_____

_____

7. How would you paraphrase Psalm 90:17 in regard to your work?

_____

_____

_____

_____

8. Our work can be an effective training ground for spiritual growth and the development of Christian character.

a. In what specific ways do you see the potential for that in your job?

_____

_____

_____

_____

_____

_____

b. What can you do to make those things happen?

_____

_____

_____

_____

_____

7
Numbering Our Days

To "spend" your life for that which is eternally valuable requires prayerful, purposeful forethought followed by deliberate choices of action. The reward is a sense of integration and meaning infused into daily life.

1. It's easy to muddle through life following the cues of everyone around us.

   a. What does the Bible teach about reflection and godly planning?

   Proverbs 16:3 _____

   _____

   _____

   _____

   Proverbs 24:3 _____

   _____

   _____

   Isaiah 32:8 _____

   _____

   _____

b. What motivation does 1 Peter 1:17-19 provide to stop and assess what we are giving our lives to?

_____

_____

_____

_____

_____

_____

2. In Ecclesiastes, Solomon gives us the benefit of learning from his exploits and search for meaning and fulfillment in life.

a. Record in the chart what he learned.

	What he explored	What he discovered
By wisdom Ecclesiastes 1:12-18		
By pleasure Ecclesiastes 2:1-11		
By materialism Ecclesiastes 2:17-23		

b. What conclusion did he finally draw? Ecclesiastes 12:13-14

_____

_____

_____

_____

_____

_____

3. In Psalm 90, Moses voices a prayer that is his reflection on meaning and purpose in life.

a. Verses 1-2
What is the overarching truth Moses mentions here, the truth he uses to preface all that follows?

_____

_____

_____

_____

b. Verses 3-6
How does he describe the brevity of life?

_____

_____

_____

_____

_____

c. Verses 7-11

Here Moses considers what it might be like to stand before the omniscient scrutiny of God's eyes. As Moses anticipates accountability before the Lord, what does he remind himself of?

_____

_____

_____

_____

_____

_____

d. Verse 12

What is his conclusion?

_____

_____

_____

_____

e. Verses 14-17

In light of this, what does Moses request of the Lord?

_____

_____

_____

_____

_____

f. How would you conclude the following prayer: "Lord, You are all that is, all that matters. The number of my days is very few, and someday I will give an account for the stewardship of my life."

_____

_____

_____

_____

_____

_____

_____

4. Our lives are easily consumed with the temporal, yet God would turn our attention to that which *lasts,* that which has permanence because it is a reflection of Him.

a. What do the following verses reveal as everlasting?

Psalm 33:11 _____

_____

_____

_____

1 Peter 1:23-25 _____

_____

_____

_____

1 John 2:17 _____

_____

_____

_____

b. Take a few moments to meditate on and personalize
   1 John 2:17.

_____

_____

_____

_____

_____

c. How would you complete this sentence: In my life, the
   "lusts" that perenially attract me and yet are fleeting,
   temporal, and of no lasting importance are

_____

_____

_____

_____

_____

_____

_____

d. Aleksandr Solzhenitsyn wrote, "We always pay dearly for chasing after what is cheap."[1] How would you paraphrase that idea?

_____

_____

_____

_____

_____

_____

5 Much advice is offered and exhortation given to "increase your capacity" and "develop your full potential." How do the following verses offer that hope biblically for the person who follows God?

Psalm 18:36 _____

_____

_____

_____

Psalm 84:5-7 _____

_____

_____

Psalm 119:32 _____

_____

_____

6. Take some time to think over the last few years. Use the following questions to evaluate what is really important to you—thus, what your life purpose/purposes might be.

a. Where and how did you invest your discretionary time?

_____

_____

_____

_____

_____

_____

b. Where and how did you invest your money?

_____

_____

_____

_____

_____

c. What most often drained your emotional energy?

_____

_____

_____

_____

_____

d. What do you find your thoughts turning to repeatedly?

_____

_____

_____

_____

_____

_____

7. As an application from this chapter, make a date with yourself to invest two to eight hours in establishing a life pur-
   pose/purposes and corresponding one- and five-year goals.

_____

_____

_____

_____

_____

_____

_____

NOTE
1. Aleksandr Solzhenitsyn, *Gulag Archipelago 2* (New York: Harper and Row, 1975), page 565.

8
Temporal Versus Eternal Wealth

Martin Luther said that there are three necessary conversions: the mind, the heart, and the purse. Certainly the way we use money can accurately mirror the spiritual state of our heart.

1. Everywhere we turn in our modern culture, money is projected as the answer to life's problems, the panacea for all our ills. The Bible is far more realistic.

   a. Consider Proverbs 23:4-5 and Ecclesiastes 5:10-11. What do they teach about money and material wealth?

   _____

   _____

   _____

   _____

   _____

   b. What does Solomon declare about the goal mentioned in Proverbs 30:8-9, and why does he say that?

   _____

   _____

   _____

   _____

2. A sizable portion of Paul's first letter to Timothy is an explanation of the relationship between money and godliness. Read carefully Paul's instructions in 1 Timothy 6:6-19.

a. In verses 9 and 10, Paul's point is so crucial that he repeats it twice in different words. What is he trying to communicate so strongly?

_____

_____

_____

_____

_____

_____

b. Look at verse 11. After instructing us to flee from the allure of becoming wealthy, Paul lists quite specifically what we should pursue. Paraphrase those things by completing this thought: God considers it worth my time and energy to concentrate on

_____

_____

_____

_____

_____

_____

_____

c. Do you sense God prompting you to pursue one thing in particular at this point in your life? If so, which one?

_____

_____

_____

_____

d. Three times, in verses 12, 16, and 19, Paul weaves in the theme of eternity and an eternal perspective. Why does the reality of eternity have such bearing on the question of money? What is Paul trying repeatedly to turn our attention to?

_____

_____

_____

_____

_____

_____

e. How would you summarize God's directives for "rich" people?

_____

_____

_____

_____

_____

f. What do you think is the difference between placing our hope in money or "things" and placing our hope in God, who out of His grace supplies our needs?

_____

_____

_____

_____

_____

_____

g. Compare 1 Timothy 6:19 with Luke 12:15. In both of these verses, what is the Bible saying concerning *life*?

_____

_____

_____

_____

_____

3. a. We tend to think of the sin in Sodom as perverted sensual desire. Describe the deeper sin of the people of Sodom, as seen in Ezekiel 16:49.

_____

_____

_____

_____

b. The Bible gives us counsel on how we can keep from falling into the trap of hoarding wealth and becoming oblivious to the needs of others, especially Christians. Consider the following verses (and any others you feel are pertinent) as you formulate principles for preventing a greedy spirit and lifestyle.

1 Samuel 30:22-24 _____

_____

_____

_____

_____

Psalm 62:10 _____

_____

_____

_____

_____

Hebrews 13:5-6 _____

_____

_____

_____

_____

4. In Luke 12:13-21, Jesus told a story of a wealthy man who exemplified greed.

a. Describe what this man was like, how he thought, what the outcome of his life was.

_____

_____

_____

_____

_____

_____

_____

_____

b. Do you think that a person has to be rather wealthy to suffer from greed? Why or why not?

_____

_____

_____

_____

_____

_____

_____

_____

5. Christ's teaching that follows His parable of the wealthy man is designed to change our mind-set and thereby prevent a greedy, acquisitive lifestyle. Read Luke 12:22-34.

   a. List as many characteristics of that changed mind-set as you can discover in the passage.

   _____

   _____

   _____

   _____

   _____

   _____

   _____

   _____

   b. If you and I adopt this outlook, how will it keep us from becoming like the man Jesus described?

   _____

   _____

   _____

   _____

   _____

   _____

6. In the New Testament, we see how God uses our giving of material wealth to further His Kingdom in the world and in us as well. Read carefully 2 Corinthians 9:6-15.

a. What characteristics of biblical giving can you find in
   these verses?

_____

_____

_____

_____

_____

b. Giving is not just one way. What does the giver receive?

_____

_____

_____

_____

c. Should a person give to God after his own needs are suffi-
   ciently met? Or should he give first and then trust God to
   make his resources sufficient to meet his needs? Support
   your view from Scripture.

_____

_____

_____

_____

_____

_____

7. Do you think that it's possible to give money in order to keep from giving yourself—your time, energy, or reputation—to God in deeper, more profound ways? Why or why not?

_____

_____

_____

_____

_____

_____

_____

_____

8. The fourth chapter of Philippians includes two often-quoted promises: "I can do all things through Him who strengthens me" (verse 13) and "My God shall supply all your needs according to His riches in glory in Christ Jesus" (verse 19).

   a. Consider each promise in its context. According to verses 10-13, in what circumstances did Paul specifically claim the sufficiency of God's power?

   _____

   _____

   _____

   _____

   _____

b. Read verses 14-19. What prompted Paul to remind the Philippians that they could count on God's provision?

_____

_____

_____

_____

_____

_____

_____

c. How can you apply these two promises in your life in light of the meaning of their context?

_____

_____

_____

_____

_____

_____

_____

_____

_____

9. Considering what you have studied concerning money and material wealth, how would you complete this sentence: God will never use money in my life to

_____

_____

_____

_____

_____

_____

10. As you have reflected on God's Word in this chapter, have you felt led to begin, change, or stop a particular action? Explain your answer.

_____

_____

_____

_____

_____

_____

_____

_____

_____

_____

9
Developing Spiritual Eyesight

Modern man values that which can be seen, touched, or heard. But as Christians, our ability to determine what is truly valuable in God's eyes depends largely on our ability to see beyond the material and the tangible to the spiritual and the eternal.

1. In the death and resurrection of Christ, observant bystanders saw only a righteous man who died between two thieves, who was buried in a borrowed tomb, and whose body mysteriously disappeared three days later. Yet the Bible reveals the account of what actually took place in the eternal, spiritual realm.

   a. Read Hebrews 9:11-12 and 24 and then describe the spiritual events.

   _____

   _____

   _____

   _____

   _____

   _____

   _____

   _____

b. Confidence in this spiritual reality can have personal, practical ramifications in our lives. How would you explain what those are?

Hebrews 9:13-14 _____

_____

_____

Hebrews 10:14 _____

_____

_____

Hebrews 10:22-24 _____

_____

_____

2. God's blessings are primarily spiritual in nature. In Psalm 16, David speaks of some of the blessings of knowing God. Read verses 5-11 and describe those blessings.

_____

_____

_____

_____

_____

_____

_____

3. It's easy to view this world as *reality,* while the world to come is but a weak *substitute* designed to console people who are deprived of joys the temporal world offers. Yet the Bible reverses that view: the heavenly, the eternal, is reality, of which the present world can give us only a mild foretaste, even as taped music is a poor substitute for a live orchestra.

   a. Look at 2 Corinthians 4:17-18 and explain how the Bible presents this paradox.

   _____

   _____

   _____

   _____

   _____

   _____

   b. How does recognizing this help us loosen our grip on the material world and make it possible for us to *enjoy* without *clinging*?

   _____

   _____

   _____

   _____

   _____

   _____

   _____

   _____

   _____

4. a. A person's spiritual insight determines his value system. Use the verses below to contrast the value system of the Pharisees with what God considers important.

The Pharisees—Luke 16:15, John 12:42-43

_____

_____

_____

_____

God—1 Samuel 15:22-23, Isaiah 66:2

_____

_____

_____

_____

_____

b. How can these particular verses, which represent two different value systems, influence a choice you are facing?

_____

_____

_____

_____

_____

_____

5. In the discourse of John 6, Christ tried repeatedly to reveal Himself in spiritual dimensions to a group of disciples who were totally unable or unwilling to see. Read John 6:30-40.

a. What was the multitude seeking?

_____

_____

_____

_____

_____

b. What did Jesus continually direct them to?

_____

_____

_____

_____

_____

_____

6. a. Consider the examples of Noah and Abraham, two men who lived by faith in unseen spiritual realities. What motivated each of these men?

Noah—Hebrews 11:7 _____

_____

_____

_____

Abraham—Hebrews 11:8-10 _____

_____

_____

_____

b. Read Hebrews 12:1-2. How would you describe the spiritual vision that should motivate each of us?

_____

_____

_____

_____

_____

7. *Idolatry,* a word used primarily in the Old Testament, means seeking fulfillment, deliverance, or a sense of significance from the material world rather than from our relationship with God.

   a. What do these verses reveal about seeking to have our needs met in an idolatrous way?

   1 Samuel 12:20-21 _____

   _____

   _____

   Isaiah 41:29 _____

   _____

   _____

Jeremiah 2:8 _____

_____

_____

b. What results from this approach to life?

Psalm 115:8 _____

_____

_____

_____

Isaiah 44:20 _____

_____

_____

_____

Jeremiah 2:8 _____

_____

_____

_____

Jonah 2:8 _____

_____

_____

_____

c. In light of these truths, what conviction did David adamantly express in Psalm 101:3?

_____

_____

_____

_____

_____

8. How could you personally apply David's statement in your own life, turning your attention from the substitutes of this world to the eternal realities of the Spirit?

_____

_____

_____

_____

_____

_____

_____

_____

10
For Generations to Come

Through our children, God gives us the opportunity to influence future generations of people for Him. But in order to do that, we must think of the future so that we are motivated to take advantage of everything the present affords us with our children.

If you do not have children, answer these questions as best you can in light of children you may have in the future.

1. What do the following verses suggest about our lives and the future of those who will follow us?

Deuteronomy 6:1-3 _____

_____

_____

_____

Acts 2:38-39 _____

_____

_____

_____

Acts 13:33 _____

_____

_____

2. Our actions in the present carry consequences for good or ill for those who follow us. Describe what those repercussions are.

Exodus 34:7 _____

_____

_____

_____

Numbers 14:32-33 _____

_____

_____

_____

Psalm 37:26 _____

_____

_____

_____

Psalm 103:17-18 _____

_____

_____

_____

3. a. As we try to communicate the faith to our children, what does God particularly want us to teach them? In the following verses, note the insight given for *how* that message is best communicated as well as for *what* we should teach our children.

Deuteronomy 6:4-9 _____

_____

_____

_____

_____

Psalm 78:5-8 _____

_____

_____

_____

_____

b. In what practical ways can a parent effectively demonstrate to a child what it means to put his or her confidence
in God?

_____

_____

_____

_____

_____

_____

4. The younger generation of Hebrews who wandered in the wilderness and followed Joshua into the Promised Land were faithful to Moses' exhortations to keep God's covenant and His commandments. According to Judges 2:10, in what ways did they fall short in passing on God's truth to their children?

_____

_____

_____

_____

_____

5. God wants us to describe our personal pilgrimage of faith to our children.

   a. Look at the way that David described his spiritual journey (Psalm 40:1-3) and then take a few moments to decide how you can explain yours on a child's level of understanding.

   _____

   _____

   _____

   _____

   _____

   _____

   _____

   _____

b. Think of yourself as a Hebrew parent who has been brought out of Egypt and into the Promised Land. What would Deuteronomy 6:20-23 and Joshua 4:21-24 encourage you to share about your past?

_____

_____

_____

_____

_____

_____

6. At one particularly low point in Israel's history, when the people were captive in Egypt as slaves, Pharaoh decreed that any son born to a Hebrew family must be thrown into the Nile River. God used the faith of two parents and the compassion of Pharaoh's own daughter to preserve the person (Moses) who would eventually lead God's people out of Egyptian enslavement.

a. Read Exodus 2:1-10 and Hebrews 11:23. In what ways do you see the faith of Moses' parents demonstrated?

_____

_____

_____

_____

_____

_____

b. Look also at Hebrews 11:24-26. What do you think Moses' parents might have been able to communicate spiritually in order to foster Moses' commitment to God? (Moses could have stayed with his parents until he was weaned, possibly his first three or four years.)

_____

_____

_____

_____

_____

7. The story of Eli and his sons, Hophni and Phinehas, presents a more sobering, unfortunate account. Read 1 Samuel 2:12-17 and 22-34.

a. Describe what Eli's sons were like.

_____

_____

_____

_____

b. What principles of God-fearing parenting did Eli violate?

_____

_____

_____

_____

_____

8. In spite of all their efforts, many parents experience the pain of a prodigal child. Read such a story in Luke 15:11-24.

a. What did this father have to endure as he helplessly watched his son take the wrong course?

_____

_____

_____

_____

_____

b. In what ways did God intervene in the son's life?

_____

_____

_____

_____

_____

c. Look carefully at verses 20-24. What does the passage tell you about the father's heart?

_____

_____

_____

_____

_____

d. What played a part in the prodigal's return home?

_____

_____

_____

_____

_____

_____

9. When the demands of life crowd in, why do you think it is so easy to neglect our family first, to give them our leftover time and energy?

_____

_____

_____

_____

_____

_____

10. In Deuteronomy 6:6, Moses reminded God's children that God's truth—His values—must first of all be enshrined in *our* hearts before we can have any hope of passing on a spiritual heritage. Thus, we must consider the question, What is really significant and important to me?

    This week try to get some objective feedback to that question about yourself by talking to your children, your spouse, or a good friend.

a. In light of that feedback, as well as what you studied here, how would you complete this thought: By the witness of my life and lips, I feel I effectively communicate the following aspects of biblical truth and values:

_____

_____

_____

_____

_____

_____

b. In what areas do you feel the need for improvement, and what steps could you take in that direction?

_____

_____

_____

_____

_____

_____

_____

_____

11
An Eternal
Hope

Trials and difficulties are facts of life. But as Christians, godly responses in the face of such obstacles will bring eternal gain.

1. Augustine said that God had one Son without sin, but no son without trials. Certainly the Bible bears witness to that fact. The life of the Apostle Paul reveals the juxtaposition of victory and opposition, adversity even in the midst of triumph.

   a. Record the pattern of victory and opposition in the chart below.

	Victory	Opposition
Cyprus	Acts 13:6-7,12	Acts 13:8-11
Pisidian Antioch	Acts 13:44,48-49	Acts 13:45,50
Iconium	Acts 14:1	Acts 14:2,5-6
Lystra	Acts 14:8-12	Acts 14:19-21

b. As you correlate your observations with 1 Peter 4:12-13, how would you express the principle of the Christian life that you see here?

_____

_____

_____

_____

_____

_____

2. Not all our difficulties, however, are the result of suffering for our faith. Sometimes we struggle with what appears to be the general unfairness of life—good things happen to bad people and bad things happen to good people. We question the goodness of a righteous God, even as Asaph did in Psalm 73. Read the entire psalm to get an overview of his struggles.

a. What basic presupposition was Asaph trying to confirm in spite of what appeared to be contrary evidence?

Verse 1 _____

_____

_____

_____

_____

_____

b. What two observations directly challenged Asaph's basic presupposition?

Verses 2-12 _____

_____

_____

_____

Verses 13-14 _____

_____

_____

c. What truths helped Asaph resolve his mental conflict?

Verses 16-18 _____

_____

_____

_____

Verses 25-28 _____

_____

_____

_____

_____

d. What conclusion do you think Asaph came to?

_____

_____

_____

_____

e. How would you define God's goodness?

_____

_____

_____

_____

3. The Bible is an honest book. Its pages reveal those who have experienced the gamut of negative emotions, the very depths of discouragement.

   a. Look at three such people and record their mental struggles and the accompanying emotions.

   Job

   Job 23:8-9,15 _____

   _____

   _____

   _____

   _____

   _____

Jeremiah

Lamentations 3:1-18 _____

_____

_____

_____

_____

_____

_____

Jesus Christ

Prophetically—Psalm 22:1-2,11-18
Matthew 26:38-42

_____

_____

_____

_____

_____

_____

_____

_____

b. Do you feel that discouragement and depression (the companion of prolonged discouragement) are results of sin? Why or why not, or in what circumstances?

_____

_____

_____

_____

_____

_____

4. The children of Israel experienced some hard times in their journey from Egypt to the Promised Land. Read the account in Exodus 17:1-7 of their complaints about the lack of water.

Is this merely an inside look at human frustrations expressed in a difficult situation, or were the children of Israel questioning something? For additional insight, you might read the Bible's commentary on a similar incident in Psalm 78:17-20.

_____

_____

_____

_____

_____

_____

5. What do these Old Testament and New Testament passages reveal about the reasons God allows difficult periods in our lives and the benefits we can derive from those times?

	The reasons	The potential benefits
Deuter-onomy 8:2-5,16-17		
Hebrews 12:3-11		

6. Life in a fallen world inevitably brings each of us a measure of trials and heartaches. Sometimes our only choice is the response we will adopt in the face of difficulty. Describe the responses of the following people:

Daniel's three friends, as they faced the fiery furnace—
Daniel 3:16-18

_____

_____

_____

_____

_____

_____

Job, as he lost all he had—Job 1:20-22

_____

_____

_____

_____

_____

Jesus, as He looked toward death on the cross—John 12:27-28

_____

_____

_____

_____

_____

7. In the midst of great trials and difficulties and the subsequent temptation to give in to discouragement, what truths did the men listed below choose to focus their thoughts and wills on?

Jeremiah, as he faithfully prophesied the truth to a rebellious people who focused their anger and resentment on him—Lamentations 3:21-25

_____

_____

_____

_____

David, as he lived in exile, on the run from Saul—Psalm
59:16-17 and Psalm 63:1-5

_____

_____

_____

_____

_____

Habakkuk, as he glimpsed the coming judgment on God's
people—Habakkuk 3:17-19

_____

_____

_____

_____

8. a. Consider a difficulty or trial you are currently facing. How
can you avoid the response exhibited by the children of
Israel in Exodus?

_____

_____

_____

_____

_____

_____

_____

b. As you think about the various responses of people in this chapter, which truths might be particularly helpful to you in your situation?

_____

_____

_____

_____

_____

_____

_____

c. How could you apply them to your circumstances?

_____

_____

_____

_____

_____

_____

_____

12
The Promise
of the Future

Eternity will involve some measure of accountability for our present life, as well as eternal reward. Both are valid scriptural motivations for resolute commitment to following Christ.

1. Part of the human condition seems to be the struggle to believe that God is just, and will demonstrate His goodness and mercy toward His children. How do the following verses demonstrate this kind of struggle?

Psalm 73:13-14 _____

_____

_____

_____

Isaiah 40:27 _____

_____

_____

_____

Isaiah 49:4 _____

_____

_____

Malachi 3:14 _____

_____

_____

_____

_____

2. What do the verses in the chart reveal about God's goodness and His desire to bless us? What particular dangers are referred to in some of the verses?

	God's goodness	Dangers
Psalm 27:13		
Romans 8:18		
Galatians 6:9		
Ephesians 6:8		
Hebrews 10:35-36		

3. Trials and suffering reveal the genuineness of our faith, for which God promises to reward us.

a. What causes for rejoicing are revealed in James 1:2-4 and 1 Peter 1:6-9?

_____

_____

_____

_____

_____

_____

_____

_____

b. What did confidence in God's reward enable Jesus to do? Hebrews 12:2

_____

_____

_____

_____

_____

_____

_____

4. According to 2 Corinthians 4:7-11, what reward do we experience in the present as the result of following Christ?

_____

_____

_____

_____

_____

_____

_____

5. In Revelation 22:12, Christ said, "Behold, I am coming quickly, and My reward is with Me, to render to every man according to what he has done." It is common to conclude that those rewards are based on the results we achieve for Him in this life.

Read 1 Corinthians 3:8,11-15 and 1 Corinthians 4:5 to decide what the basis is for Heaven's rewards.

_____

_____

_____

_____

_____

_____

_____

_____

6. In terms of Heaven's rewards, the Bible speaks specifically of five crowns.

   a. Read the passages in the chart to determine the basis of each reward and the prerequisite for receiving it.

	The basis for the reward	The prerequisite
The crown of victory 1 Corinthians 9:24-27		
The crown of exalting Philippians 4:1; 1 Thessalonians 2:19-20		
The crown of righteousness 2 Timothy 4:6-8		
The crown of life James 1:12		
The crown of glory 1 Peter 5:1-4		

b. As you think about what it means to live for Christ, do you think these crowns or rewards are particularly appropriate? Why or why not?

_____

_____

_____

_____

_____

_____

7. What do the following verses reveal about the relationship between motivation and the sure prospect of standing before a righteous God to give an account of your life?

2 Corinthians 5:9-11 _____

_____

_____

_____

Hebrews 12:28-29 _____

_____

_____

_____

1 John 2:28 _____

_____

_____

8. Considering the reality of giving an account for your life and the prospect of eternal reward, how does this knowledge affect your motivation to follow Christ?

_____

_____

_____

_____

_____

_____

_____

_____

BIBLE STUDY MATERIALS FROM NAVPRESS

BIBLE STUDY SERIES
DESIGN FOR DISCIPLESHIP—seven books and leader's guide
EXPERIENCING GOD—three books
Discovering God's Will
Experiencing God's Attributes
Experiencing God's Presence
GOD IN YOU—six books and leader's guide
GOD'S DESIGN FOR THE FAMILY—two books
LEARNING TO LIVE—six books
LIFECHANGE—studies of books of the Bible
STUDIES IN CHRISTIAN LIVING—six books

TOPICAL BIBLE STUDIES
Becoming a Woman of Excellence
Celebrate the Seasons!
God, Man, and Jesus Christ
Homemaking
In His Name
On Holy Ground
Overcoming
Spiritual Fitness—also leader's guide
Think It Through
To Walk and Not Grow Weary

BIBLE STUDIES WITH COMPANION BOOKS
Essentials of Discipleship
The Freedom of Obedience
Friends and Friendship
Honesty, Morality, and Conscience
Marriage Takes More Than Love
The Power of Commitment
The Practice of Godliness
The Pursuit of Holiness
True Fellowship (companion study to *The Crisis of Caring*)

RESOURCES
Explore the Bible Yourself
Leader's Guide for Evangelistic Bible Studies
The Navigator Bible Studies Handbook
Topical Memory System—available in KJV/NIV and NASB/RSV